THE CHANGING

Easington

BOOK ONE

Barry Davis and Brian Little

SERIES
NUMBER
45

Robert Boyd
PUBLICATIONS

Published by
Robert Boyd Publications
260 Colwell Drive
Witney, Oxfordshire OX8 7LW

First published 2000

Copyright © Barry Davis, Brian Little and
Robert Boyd Publications

ISBN: 1 899536 54 X

Printed and bound in Great Britain at
The Alden Press, Oxford

TITLES IN THE *CHANGING FACES* SERIES

Do you want to publish a book?

It is not as difficult as you might think. The publisher of this book provides a service to individuals and organisations, large and small.

Advice can be given on all facets of book production.

If you have a project you would like to discuss why not contact:

Robert Boyd
PRINTING & PUBLISHING SERVICES
260 Colwell Drive
Witney
Oxfordshire
OX8 7LW

Contents

Cover illustrations

Front: V.E. or V.J. Day in Addison Road.

Back: Midland Red's Easington B1 Service.
(Courtesy of Eddie Turvey)

Acknowledgements

We would like to thank all those who have helped at different stages in the development of this book by talking about their memories etc. of Easington or by loaning photographs and documents. A considerable number of images have come from my own collection (Barry Davis)

In particular our thanks go to Gertie Ashby, Julie Ashworth, Banbury Operatic Society, Jesse and the late Stan Brown, Archie Buzzard, Henry and Jean Chester, Bob Cobill, Arthur Coleman, Andy Cox, Mike Dancer, Beryl Davis, Lew Gray, Malcolm Hearne, David Hedderley, Charles Herbert, Walter McCanna, Frank and Ellen Maycock, John Matthews, Bob Milsom, Joan Moseley, John Neale, Elsie Payne, Pat Rix, Vera Stanton, John Stokes, Mrs Ivy Toms, Eddie Turvey, Mrs Wise, Ken Young and Beazer (Strategic Land).

Thanks also go to the Banbury Guardian for permission to reproduce some of their photographs and to Jean Davis for reading and commenting on the text and producing the up to date map of the area.

Preface

This book is about the southwest corner of Banbury. In common with the volumes on the town centre and Grimsbury, it seeks to identify the people and the processes responsible for the changes in its character.

Easington is bounded by the pre M40 main road to Oxford (formerly the A41T and the A423), by the A361 Bloxham Road and, on its western margins, by an ancient track called Salt Lane.

The district is mainly residential but there are three schools, two church buildings and some small shops serving especially local needs.

Our text is enlivened by interviews with people who have spent varying proportions of their lives in Easington. Recollections and illustrations combine to show that despite the comparatively short period of history of most of the area, there is a treasury of memories and therefore some tales to tell.

Introduction

The Changing Faces of Easington is a first book and not an exhaustive study. Tudor Hall School, the Horton Hospital, Grange Road Methodist Church, Banbury School and Banbury Rugby Club are all supremely well covered in other publications.

Another major consideration was the availability of photographs. Inevitably the overall picture for the area is patchy and undoubtedly some family possessions have disappeared for whatever reasons.

As with Grimsbury, the district of Easington commenced with farm related elements and has retained some kind of agricultural boundary right up to the present day. There is now no rural gap between Easington and Bodicote village to the south but farmland does border the western perimeter.

Retail activities in the form of small shops occur in and close to Horton View and Timms Road.

Education is represented by Harriers Ground School and two secondary establishments, namely Banbury and Blessed George Napier Schools. The last of these two is of Roman Catholic foundation.

Religious worship is available at St. Hughs in Ruskin Road (Anglican), Grange Road Chapel (Methodist), and in Banbury School (Banbury Free Church).

Education and Religion form an ideal partnership for one chapter in Easington 'Book II' Each has a place within this first volume but is not treated at great length.

The origins and early growth of Easington

The Oxford Road from its junction with High Town Road looking towards Bodicote.

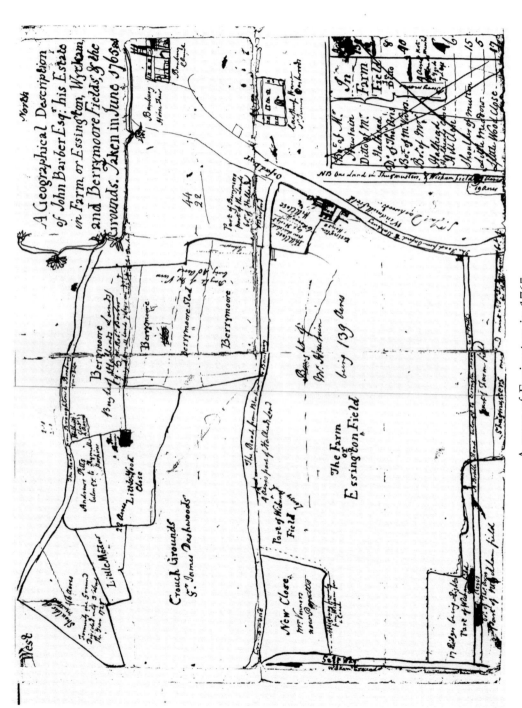

A map of Easington in 1765.

By the final decade of the nineteenth century, whereas Grimsbury (Banbury's neighbour to the east) was well developed, the area linked to the name Easington was a mosaic of grass and arable land given over to farming. There were large acreages such as Middle Field and Farm Field but also smaller and specifically named plots, notably Salt way, Furlong and Shugmaster Piece. The Furlong stretch related to an old drove road whereas Shugmaster was the name of a farm. William Denchfield was linked to land in this area.

Letter relating to purchase of land in the Bloxham Road from the Risley family.

Easington Farmhouse and the Victorian water tower.

On the northern and eastern margins of this farmed land and bounded by the Bloxham and Oxford Roads was Easington House and Farm. Originally it was the home farm of the Bishop of Lincoln but by the fifteenth century such was the inconvenient size of his diocese that parts were leased to tenants. The first of these was John Danvers (about 1430) and the second William Pierson (1520) who was succeeded by the Hawtens whose main property was Calthorpe Manor. Profits from wool may have permitted the construction of Easington house but the outcome was less elaborate than Calthorpe.

At the end of the eighteenth century the farmhouse was repaired and extended.

In 1857 land to the southeast of Easington Farmhouse was leased by the Risleys, (the then landowners), to the Banbury Water Company Ltd. who wanted to establish a reservoir. The Rev. Cotton, Susannah (his wife) and Halford Cotton Risley were Deddington based but had connections with a family called Barber and their land interests in this part of Easington.

A detailed account of the farm appears in a sale brochure produced by Humbert and Flint for an auction at the Red Lion Hotel, High Street, Banbury in May 1919.

LOT I

(Coloured Pink on Plan).

The Valuable Freehold Estate

KNOWN AS

Easington Farm.

Is situate on the outskirts of, and adjoining, the important and thriving Market Town of Banbury,
and the whole lies within the Borough Boundary

The Town is situated on the Main Great Western London to Birmingham Line, by which
London may be reached in two hours, and Birmingham in a little over the hour. It is also the
terminus of the London and North Western Railway, Banbury Branch, which links up Banbury
with the London to Oxford Route *via* Verney Junction, and it can also be reached from London
by the Great Central Railway Branch Line from Woodford.

BANBURY

is a Market Town, the centre of a large Agricultural
District, with great manufacturing possibilities, and
with the growth of its industries, there will be an
increased demand for Building Sites for Residences
::   ::   or Housing Schemes.   ::   ::

The Land now offered is probably the most eligible and desirable
within the Borough, with great potentialities for development as a
Building Estate.

Lot 1: Sale of the farm.

View across Easington from St. Mary's tower. Springfield Avenue can be seen in
the far distance.

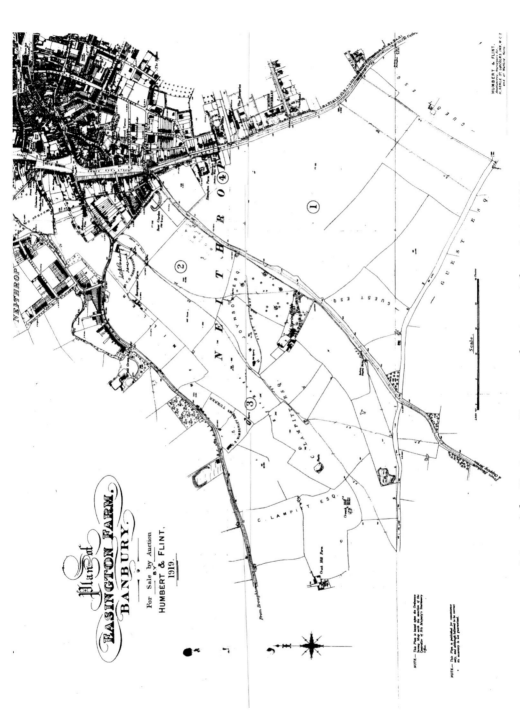

Map of the Easington Estate at the time of the sale in 1919.

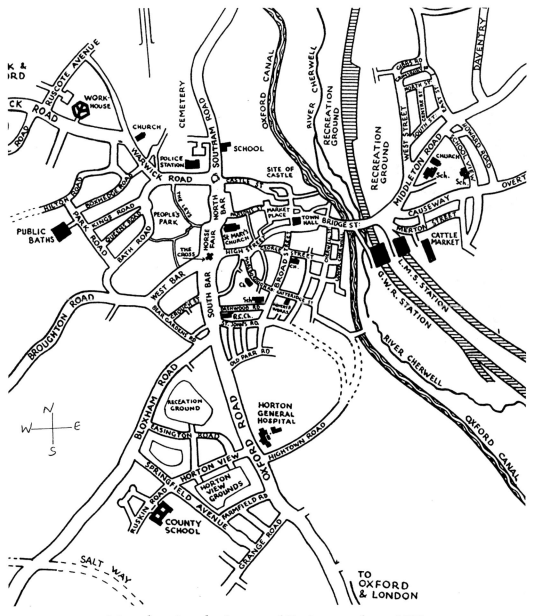

Map showing the layout of Easington about 1930.

The overall description of property and field is set in the context of the desirability of this part of Banbury. In the words of the auctioneers "the land now offered is probably the most eligible and desirable within the Borough, with great potential for development as a building estate".

Although Banbury was still perceived as a market town, a growing industrial base suggested increased demand for building sites for residences or housing

Looking up Springfield Avenue from the Bloxham Road in 1923. This was the first phase to be built.

schemes. Post World War I Banbury needed new homes to counter balance anticipated slum clearance in some more central parts such as the Cherwell Streets.

Banbury Borough Council interest in Easington came just after the war of 1914-1918 when they acquired some of the 90 acres of land. Half of this was developed by 1919 but the rest waited until 1923 and 1924.

A total of 403 Council houses were built but there was also private sector development on the west side of the Oxford Road from the water tower to Grange Road. Humphris and Sons also purchased land from the estate and one of the houses they built was 41 Bloxham Road on the corner of Bloxham Road and Harriers View.

Characteristic of Corporation dealings was the 1924 acquisition of 680 square yards of land in the space framed by Easington Road and Horton View. This had been part of the Easington Farm Estate sold by auction in 1919.

Gordon Bernard Osborne, a cycle agent and radio dealer, bought part of this plot of land. At that time the title 'future road' was used for the later Easington Road. On the opposite side of Horton View there was a short access to and from a sports field (later owned by the Northern Aluminium Company).

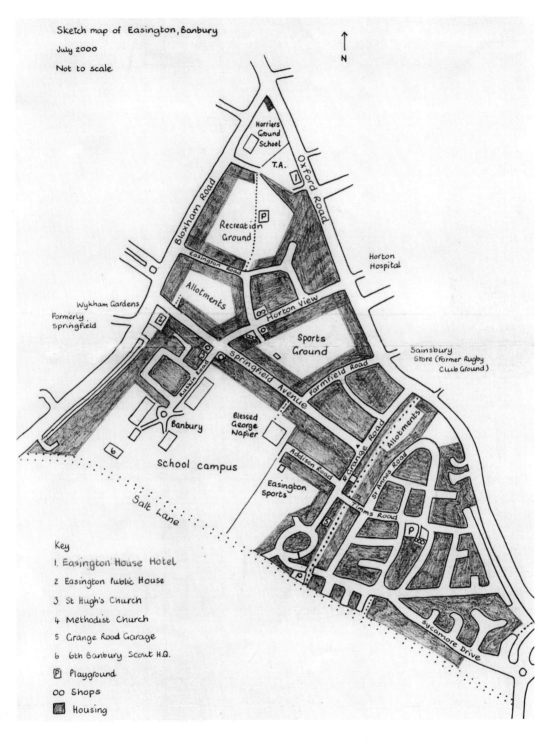

Sketch map of Easington, Banbury

July 2000

Not to scale

N

Harriers Ground School

T.A.

1

Oxford Road

Bloxham Road

P

Recreation Ground

Easington Road

Horton Hospital

Allotments

Wykham Gardens

Formerly Springfield

2

00 Horton View

Ruskin Road

3

Sports Ground

Springfield Avenue

Farmfield Road

Sainsbury Store (Former Rugby Club Ground)

Allotments

Banbury

Blessed George Napier

6

school campus

Addison Road

Grange Road

St Anne's Road

Easington Sports

4

Timms Road

5

P

P

Salt Lane

Sycamore Drive

Key

1. Easington House Hotel

2 Easington Public House

3 St Hugh's Church

4 Methodist Church

5 Grange Road Garage

6 6th Banbury Scout H.Q.

P Playground

00 Shops

Housing

Map showing the present day layout of Easington.

Fourteen years on from Osborne's site purchase, he conveyed the property built there to his wife Ivy Veronica. The home was given the name 'Verona' in recognition of the switch of ownership.

In 1925, Mr Wrigley, who was the borough surveyor, compiled a street map which was re-printed in the Banbury Guardian for April 16th. The reason, given by the editor, for its inclusion in the paper was that the Easington Estate was a little known district.

Springfield Avenue, Easington Road, St George's Crescent and Horton View combined to embrace and border the open spaces designed for public informal activity, cricket, tennis and use by the allotment holders.

Easington was our home

Beryl Davis (nee Salter) lived with her family in the wooden huts in Harriers View. These were erected about the time of World War 1 to house soldiers and their families. The view from the huts was across the Harriers Field to the Oxford Road. She remembers the noise made by the horses and gun carriages when the artillery went from the drill hall on manoeuvres. These huts remained until the end of the 1950s, beginning of the 1960s.

Mrs. Edith Salter outside the door to one of the huts in Harriers View.

Mrs. Salter and her daughters, Vera on the left and Beryl on the right, sitting in the Harriers Field (now Harriers Ground School). In the distance are the houses on the Oxford Road.

In 1923 the family moved into one of the first houses in the middle section of Springfield Avenue. The Bloxham Road end up to Ruskin Road was already built and established but beyond what is now 40 Springfield Avenue next to Buzzard's shop, it was just a muddy road with scaffolding laid along it. Horton View had not been built and Buzzard's shop came later.

40 Springfield Avenue in 1937.

When Horton View was built the council houses were constructed first at the end nearest to Springfield Avenue and then came the shops and private houses.

She remembers playing in the hay fields behind No. 40 until the Banbury County School was built. Schooling was at Dashwood Road School and the children had to walk to school by 9.00 a.m. They walked back to Easington for lunch which was between 12.00 p.m. and 2.00 p.m. and then back to school for a 4.00 p.m. finish. There was a school bus but only the Infants were allowed to travel on it. One day it was raining so hard that her mother refused to let her walk to school. When the school inspector asked her why she was absent she explained the reason. His response was 'You're not made of sugar.'

Some days Beryl was given a lift on the crossbar of Dr. Brinkworth's bicycle. He taught at Dashwood Road School in the boys section and lived in Horton View just below the shops.

SPRINGFIELD AVENUE
(Easington), from 91 Bloxham
road to 26 Grange avenue.
West side.
1 Raby Saml. Harry
3 Hobday Jas. Herbt
5 Smart Chas. Aubrey
7 Lewis Wm
9 Adams Jn. S
11 Harper Geo
13 Thorne Cyril G
15 Powell Wm. Edwd
17 Sansbury Wm. Hy
19 Buzzard Mark Wm
21 Chilton Geo. Wm
23 Bryant Cyril Chas
25 Rutter Mrs. F
27 Bletchly Regnld. Chas
29 Eels Emanuel E
31 Hartland Fredk. Geo
33 Hutchinson Victor Preston
35 Lambert Arth. Nathan
37 Maslin Albt. Ernest Wareham
39 Feagan Fredk
.... here is Horton view ....
41 Gurden Geo. Levi
43 Adams Fredk
45 Corbett Oliver Jack
47 Wain Herbt. Hy
49 Anthistle Jn. Hy
51 Betts Horace Fredk
53 Butler Fredk
55 Bayliss Fredk
57 Chilton Aubrey Thos. Rd
59 Adams Fras. Stratton
61 Jelfs Ernest Geo
63 Suckling Mrs. L
65 Jennings Geo
67 Wyatt Geo. Wm
69 Wilson Cyril Albt
71 Miles Wm. Jn. G
73 Hambridge Lawrence
75 Moore Fredk. Jn
77 Powell Ernest Wm
79 Hawtin Thos
81 Haslop Harry O
83 Charles Ernest A. J
85 Reynolds Geo
87 Hudson Thos
89 Maycock Winstan
91 Adkins Cuthbert Chas
93 Flint Chas. Hy
95 Owen Fras. Hy
97 Stevens Geo

99 Buttress Chas. A
101 Dale Wm. Thos
103 Powell Harold J
105 Astbury Jsph
.... here is Farmfield rd ....
107 Goodway Leonard S
109 Priest Sidney J
111 Ellis Geo
113 Watson Thos
115 Woodward Fras. Lawrence
117 Evans Fredk
119 Arms Percy
121 Mabbitt Albt
123 Mobbs Albt. Edwd
125 Heath Wm. Wltr
127 Clements Fredk. Jas
129 Higham Rt. Hy
131 Castle Hubert W
133 Boss Wm
135 Batchelor Jn. Hy
137 Coates Harold
139 Dudley Wltr. E
141 Wheatley Wm. Hy
143 Kearley Wm. Geo
145 Worrall Sidney
East side.
2 Clarke Bernard Chas
4 Buzzard Arth. W
6 Meadows Hy
8 Ives Albt. L
10 Watts Fred
12 Woodward Wm. Hy
14 Palmer Gerald H
16 Duffill Wm. Geo
18 Pearse Jas
20 Prescott Fredk. Jn
22 Loveday Herbt
24 Stevens Ernest Hy
26 Haynes Jn. Arth
28 Elliott Albt. Hy
30 Hobbs Ernest
32 Pyle Victor Hugo
34 Turner Mrs. Winifred, shopkpr
...........here is Ruskin rd...........
38 Barnard Arth. Geo. shopkpr
40 Salter Geo
42 Brown Saml. Jsph
44 Taylor Wm
46 Partridge Arth
48 Claridge Percy Jas
50 Pratt Fredk. Wltr
52 Plant Jn
54 Stanley Sidney Victor Jn
56 Cole Fredk

58 Bartlett Jn. Fras
60 Jones Rt. Jn
62 Atkins Albt
64 Small Horace Wm
66 Plaister Leslie Geo
68 Newman Thos. Wm
70 Horton Jn. Hy
72 Creed Albt. insur. agt
72 Creed Mrs. V. corsetière
74 Hutchings Fras. Jsph
76 Ayriss Chas
78 Stanton Wm. Ernest
80 Smith Rt. Wm
82 Tetley Mrs
84 Betts Hector Percvl
86 Kingston Albt. Harry
88 Parrish Arth. Wm
90 Cassell Regnld. Wm. Miles
92 Hibberd Wltr
94 Bowler Ernest Wm
96 Angell Cyril Hy
98 Lines Sidney Albt
100 Rayment Thos. Geo
102 Dale Fredk. Ernest
104 Simpson Rt. Geo
106 Ollerenshaw Jas
108 Jennings R
110 Thorne Geo
112 Turner Thos
114 Pickering Ernest
116 Winterburn Wm
118 Smith Mrs. Sarah
120 French Thos
122 Clark Chas
124 Howe Frank L
126 Rixon Edwin Tom
128 Jackson Jn. Hy
128 Jackson Mrs. E. G. dressn
130 Pratt Wm
132 Castle Mrs. E. J
134 Bayliss Herbt. E
136 Hazlewood Regnld. Jsph
138 Hillman Wm. Edwd
140 Sykes Alex. W
142 Sanders Jn
144 Roberts Rd. Harold
146 Amos Jas
148 Nicholls Chas
150 Green Wm. Wltr

List of residents living in Springfield Avenue in 1936 taken from a Banbury directory.

John Neale was born in 1936 at 17 Grange Road. He lived there until 1970. The war years comprised much of his childhood, he was fortunate in that there were lots of children in the near vicinity. They made much of their own entertainment and this included adapting the local environment. Hideaway camps were set up in Salt Lane hedgerows.

Immediate contact with the country meant that Golby's Farm could be reached by a track off Timms Road. John remembers 'helping' with the harvest by loading sheaves of corn on two wagons and then putting the sheaves into the threshing machine. At Halloween time the farm was a source of sugar beets or mangols which could be cut out in the manner of pumpkins; (these could not be afforded).

All this farm related activity was before allotments appeared behind Grange Road.

John went to school at Dashwood Road in Calthorpe. He walked there and back in all weathers. The school week involved links with different places in Banbury not all of which were in Easington. Dinners were provided at the Blue Bird cafe in Bridge Street.

Salt Lane today.

During the winter boys of the school played football on Easington Recreation Ground. For all children of the school, Sports day would be held on the Northern Aluminium Company ground off Horton View. Gardening lessons involved a shorter walk to Harriers school where a garden had been laid out. John left Dashwood School in 1951.

A specific memory of the war years (1939-1945) was that of an American army camp on the land which became the home of Banbury Rugby Club (now Sainsbury's superstore). People in the Grange Road area, including John's parents, used to invite Americans into their homes where small scale parties were held; on one occasion a tank sergeant joined in the party. Arising from such friendships there was an occasion when John and his sister were conveyed down the Oxford Road in a jeep and taken to the Palace Cinema in the Market Place.

The evidence of the war was right on their doorstep as tanks were parked in Farmfield Road. A remnant of this procedure could be seen at Bodicote for sometime after the war when a tank was parked close to the line of cottages on the Oxford Road just beyond the present Renault Garage.

John has very clear memories of his father who was a master tailor (like his father before him) based at home. He used to sit on a board in a small bedroom doing work for Robesons who were located in the High Street. The firm did a lot for the hunting fraternity and his father made jackets and jodhpurs.

One outcome of this work was the waste material which John took to Friswell's scrap business in an effort to raise a little pocket money.

Grange Road Methodist Chapel

During the war his father was in the Home Guard but afterwards he went to work at the Northern Aluminium Company factory in Southam Road.

John's mother did not shop in the centre of town. Instead she relied on the Easington Co-op for her main groceries. Sometimes John and his sister did the shopping and had to understand about coupons. Typical of brothers and sisters of the time they fought for the right to carry the bag.

A well remembered activity was collecting rose hips in Salt Lane. These were sold to Thompsons Chemists near the Palace Cinema in the Market Place.

Cray fishing was also popular. Little feeder streams of the Sor Brook at Bodicote yielded good quantities. Bait would be fish heads from Turner's shop in Broad Street. His mother disliked cooking crayfish so this was done by Grace Dumbleton next door.

Apples (Russets especially) could be collected from an orchard close to Haddons Farm. John thinks Haddons may have supplied Len Withey's dairy in Horton View.

Recreation was both formal and informal. Sunday meant chapel and Sunday school at Grange Road but afterwards there would be a family walk, this was sometimes quite long, for instance to Bodicote, then Bloxham and back to Easington.

Seasonal and informal pursuits also included sledging on the land sloping away from where the army camp had been sited just off the Oxford Road.

Well beyond where he lived and on the Oxford Road was Reg's Café – a wooden shack located on the site of the more recent Little Chef. It was a transport cafe with a good line in sandwiches filled with bacon.

Bob (Robin) Milsom came from Stratford to the Easington district of Banbury in 1934. He was aged three at the time of the move and spent the next twelve years with his family at 12 Grange Road where he was a near neighbour of John Neale

Beyond the western extremity of Grange Road there was the Salt Lane that so attracted John Neale and his young friends. Bob confirmed a similar interest in hedgerow camps and recalled how successfully undergrowth could envelope these hideaways.

When he and others were not in their hideaway, another attraction was the scaffolding of planks and poles used in the construction of the Timms Road buildings.

Primary schooling was not available in the area until the late forties with the opening of Harriers Ground School in Harriers View. So like John he walked to school in the Calthorpe area of town and attended St. John's Roman Catholic school. From there he progressed to the County School in Ruskin Road.

An early recollection of door to door services is that of a man on a bicycle with a churn and a ladle facility for milk deliveries. This man was distinguished by a brown smock and he wore gaiters.

There was no such matching memory for bread except in the case of tasty fresh rolls bought outside the area from Cleavers in Calthorpe Street where there was also a barber patronised by Bob.

Eagerly awaited each Saturday morning was the Chums session at the Palace Cinema. Here, between 9.00 a.m. and 12 noon, youngsters from all over the town could indulge themselves in the world of western and cartoon features.

V.E. Day group in Grange Road.

V.E. Day group in Beechfield Crescent.

Wartime, 1939-1945, brought a whole range of new experiences for children in Easington. The members of the American Army Camp came to mean a lot to Bob as indeed they did to many other youngsters in the Grange Road part of the district. Domestic shortages could be partly compensated by dipping into cardboard boxes full of sweets. Even at the conclusion of hostilities, food extras were eagerly welcomed. Some U.S. service personnel, who were known to Bob, had to dispose of massive tins of spam. He and a friend made a clean sweep of thirteen of these monster containers!

1945 meant V.E. Day celebrations. These were often arranged by individual streets. The photographs of big groups in Grange Road and Beechfield Crescent confirm this but also show that parties could overlap, as Bob appears in both pictures because of his friendship with Brian Gill of Beechfield Crescent.

Pat Rix and friends playing in Addison Road.

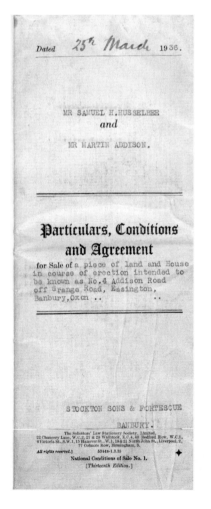

Sale agreement for 4 Addison Road.

Pat Rix's childhood was spent in Easington because her parents bought 4 Addison Road in 1936 (see lease and receipt for deposit). Their purchase was made from Michael Addison, a local builder who went out of business and whose firm was absorbed into that of Fred Timms.

Addison Road itself was very quiet (a dead end – away from the cars) and this made the street ideal for games.

Skipping was done with a rope across the whole road. Clothes lines were used. Marbles was also a popular game. The action of playing with these wore a hole that was frequently filled in by two spinsters who lived next door.

V.E or V.J. Day in Addison Road.

Shugmasters Farm.

Games outside the road were facilitated by access to farmland beyond Timms Road. In her youth, camps were popular and Salt Lane was a preferred area.

Life then (in the early forties) was fairly parochial and going to town was an adventure. Pat recalls especially that her mother had good contacts inside the International Stores. She made cakes for someone who worked there and in return received some prized items in the austerity years.

Pat remembers a house in Grange Road where a room had been converted into a workshop for making and painting lead soldiers. Literally hundreds were turned out each day. She believes the house owners were Mr. and Mrs. Butts (or Bates) and Mrs. Butts' christian name was Angela.

Martin Addison had built only part of Addison Road before his business was incorporated into that of Timms the Builders.

Walter Timms began late in 1937. An early job for his firm must have been the completion of a pair of half finished houses beyond the end of Grange Road. One of the properties had been reserved by Walter C. McCanna (now living in the Portsmouth area). It was one of a pair which became 4 and 6 Timms Road.

The McCanna Family in the garden of an early Timms Road house.

The rear of the earliest Timms Road houses looking towards Salt Lane.

Addison Road showing the three pairs of additional houses on the left.

Walter and his family moved into their new home on May 19th 1938 on what had been a field between Grange Road and the bridle path which runs between Oxford Road and Salt Lane.

At that time those who bought houses within this small extension of Easington had to cope with a raw site. The future Timms Road ended abruptly at the bridle path and the grass verges awaited levelling and seeding. The farm beyond was occupied by the Golbys and their children.

By 1940 the gardens in Grange Road had matured and blended with the surrounding rural area. All this changed with the expansion of the Timms Estate and the development of Banbury Town's cricket ground.

Bob Cobill came to Addison Road in May of 1959 and took up occupation at the northern end which was an extension of the highway and associated properties which would have been known to Pat Rix and her family.

Easington Sports Football Club had bought sufficient land to be able to permit Brackley Builders to erect three pairs of houses on the west side and two pairs of police houses to the east.

Prior to these developments a Mr. Russell had a garage and was a bus proprietor. There was also a garage in Grange Road which, in the 1960s, became home to Roy Tilstone's Coach company. Today this garage still exists, in different ownership, servicing only cars.

In 1931, Edward and Lena Bagley had built a superb five bed-roomed house in the Oxford Road near to the junction with Horton View. It merited the title of Daily Mail best designed house of the year and was a good example of the Rank I property identified by Margaret Stacey in her study of Banbury called "Tradition and Change". Professional people like Bagley, who managed the Grand Cinema in Broad Street, were the occupiers of homes in the Oxford Road.

Edward and Lena Bagley.

The Bagley's home was known as 'Coningsby' after the Lincolnshire birthplace of Lena. A feature of its garden was a custom built 'mushroom growing building'. Edward was a man for short term hobbies.

Because of the demands of professional life and an appetite for travel people worked in service at Coningsby. There were two maids, Dora and Gertie, who did the housework. Today Gertie Ashby derives huge pleasure from recalling life with the Bagleys.

Gertie first encountered Edward Bagley in 1927 and subsequently worked for him over a period of ten years. Her husband Percy was also involved as he was responsible for designing and maintaining the gardens. This was no mean task as they occupied half an acre and included an ornamental pond.

Gertie and Percy Ashby in the garden at Coningsby.

The small shop

The earliest development of shops in Easington was at two Horton View junctions; where St. George's Crescent comes in and where Springfield Avenue passes the western end of Horton View.

Horton View showing the shops on the corner of St. Georges Crescent.

It was in 1924 that Banbury Corporation became involved in the sale of plots for retail activity. A conveyance and a map of February of that year reveal the extent of the Co-operative society site. They indicate the allocation of land opposite to Leonard Rider Withey a dairyman located in the building that is now George's Second hand shop, and suggest scope for shops on the other side of Horton View. On the fourth corner there was a commitment to council houses.

By 1932 A.L.E. Williams, who was the Vicar of Banbury, was able to refer to 'a few necessary shops'. According to Kelly's Directory for that year the corner of St. George's Crescent was occupied by a baker called Harris. Next door was Percy Gilkes, newsagent.

The Harris bakery was set up in 1929 by Hubert and his father William. They had a handcart as well as a van and served Easington in addition to villages such as Shutford and Epwell. They baked bread as well as good Chelsea buns and Lardy

Harris Brothers' cart at the side of the shop in St. Georges Crescent.

Harris Brothers' van in front of the shop on Horton View.

cake. Hubert had a hen house on some allotments and eggs from here were used in his baking activities.

Hubert died in 1930 but Norman his brother continued along with William. In 1942 the business was sold to Chesters who became renowned for their fancy cakes at seven for 6d.

Chester's van outside the shop in Horton View.

Leonard Withey's dairy shop was especially attractive because of his ice creams. 1d cornets were popular with many in the area. It is likely that supplies of milk came from Bodicote Grange Farm. Leonard's delivery habits were well known. His heavy boots resounded on the pathway entrances to Easington houses. This earned him the nickname of the midnight milkman.

John Stokes had a shop in the approach to Horton View Sports ground from 1980 until recently. His choice of site was partly decided by its nearness to his home which was adjacent to the property secured in 1970.

A foot in the greengrocery business stemmed from family links with Evesham market outlets and a personal decision to handle potatoes. In order not to disappoint his regular customers, John looked east in the very dry weather of 1976 and found a reliable source in the Fen Country.

At first John Stokes made good use of his lorries for house to house distribution but he also continued to sell from the house in Horton View.

John Stokes' shop nearest, Elegance the hairdressers centre and Michael Louch Butcher on the right hand end.

John's shop was an extension of the property that was previously in the hands of the Banbury and District Co-operative Society, whose manager originally lived in the house where today Michael Louch has his butchers shop.

In 1981 David Mumford started the first butchery business. In 1992 Michael Louch bought Mumford's business. Next door Margaret Stokes set up 'Hair by Elegance' in association with Sheila Hicks. Earlier in her career, she had been manager of Wincotts salon in South Bar. Whilst there she was responsible for the hair styles of seven mayor's wives. At the Easington salon, a valued customer was the recently deceased Ethel Usher of Winter Gardens fame.

Reflecting on his retailing time in Easington, John Stokes felt that his business had been very much affected by the movement away from traditional meals served with three vegetables.

Up to five years ago he was still selling bags of coal but the declining number of coal fires killed this trade. Before his time, the Co-op had sold coal as well as petrol, the full range of groceries and in the later years was licenced to sell spirits.

There were over the years a number of other small businesses in Horton View as this selection of adverts show.

Additional shop provision was in Springfield Avenue at the corner with Ruskin Road.

Mrs. Barnard standing in the shop doorway.

The shop now known as Buzzards in Springfield Avenue was built about 1930 by Alfred Simms the brother of Ellen Barnard (nee Simms).

Ellen married Arthur Barnard and she can be seen here standing at the door to the shop. It sold much the same items as it does to day, groceries, fruit and vegetables, but every thing was sold across the counter as opposed to self-service.

Arthur and Ellen had a daughter Hilda who married Mark Buzzard. They continued to run the shop and were later joined by one of their four sons, Peter. Today the shop is looked after by Peter and his wife Joan.

Robert, one of Mark and Hilda's other sons, also followed in the retail trade at Trinders toy shop in Broad Street. Here he can be seen on a penny farthing on the forecourt of Buzzards shop.

The Easington Hotel was built in 1929 and the licence for the hotel was transferred on December 1st 1929 on the closure of the Fox in the Market Place. The Hotel was built by Hunt Edmunds on land they had bought at a cost of £250. Shortly after the Hotel was opened a postcard was produced for W. Gunn who was the landlord from 1932-1933.

This view of the gardens is taken from approximately the corner of today's car park about where it meets Springfield Avenue. The area at the back of the hotel that today is the lounge bar was originally a functions room hence the advertising on the card saying parties catered for.

Various societies, groups and wedding parties used the function room for dinners and parties.

THE HOTEL AND GARDEN

The photograph below shows some of the bell ringers who attended the Banbury Branch of Church Bellringers Annual Dinner c 1959. Jeff Hankin lived in Horton View and Richard Bentley in Wykham Place. Both were ringers at St. Mary's Parish Church, Banbury. This was a regular venue for the ringers for a number of years. The dinner was usually followed by a variety of party games.

Back row left to right: H. L. Roper, ?, ? Joe. Stretton, ?, ? , Cooke, Cooke, ?, ?, Ann Bennett, Roland Bennett, ?, Dina Bentley. *Front row left to right:* Alice Stretton, ?, Mick Gregory, ?, ?, John Sayers, Barry Davis, Jeff Hankin, Richard Bentley.

Religion and Education

St. Hugh's Church

Built partly through public subscription within the Easington district, St. Hugh's Church held its opening meeting of the Board of Managers on January 11th 1933.

The Rev. South was the priest in charge for the first year and encouraged all aspects of church life. With no spare capacity at the Ruskin Road premises, the Drill Hall on the town side of Easington Recreation Ground was utilised for Sunday school. A Miss Ginger played the piano there and also the organ at St Hughs.

In these early days finances were healthy and this inspired management members to spend 12/- on curtains and to devote funds to fencing off some land to the west of the church.

Although services were given priority, the Board recognised that the growth of the suburb might create demand for a wide range of hall uses. There was potential for a lot of work for Mr. Harper of Beechfield Crescent who was the first caretaker. His weekly salary of 8/- could be supplemented by 2/6d a month for window cleaning and between 2/6d and 3/6d for each event accepted.

The Rev. Edwards was priest in charge for the five years between 1934 and 1938. He developed both the spiritual and pastoral sides of the church. Especially

Sam Franklin and his wife celebrate their Ruby wedding. Sam played the organ at St. Hughs for many years.

notable were harvest festivals when Mr. Harris, the Horton View baker, made appropriate contributions. Apart from five little loaves and two fishes, he produced a huge item in the shape of a sheaf of corn with a mouse running up it.

In 1936 Kimberleys of Banbury constructed a front wall with railings at a cost of £23-10-0d. At this time there was a field at the rear of St. Hughs but this was considered unsuitable for fete purposes and so thoughts turned towards the Springfield Hotel which was off the Bloxham Road.

The fete of 1936 was a typical example of these occasions. There was help within the St. Hugh's organisation in order to cover a wide range of activities which included bowling for the pig, hoop-la, children's races, a treasure hunt and open air whist. More elaborate still was a proposed tennis competition. The organisation of this was entrusted to Miss Bernard Smith but sadly there were insufficient entries.

A fancy dress competition was included in the itinerary and entrants were required to muster at St. Hugh's Church Hall and then march to the fete ground headed by a band. At the end of the day the church had made £41 profit.

Some of the children in Mrs Salter's Easington Poorah band about 1937.

Each year on the day of the fete a dance was held in the Church Hall. In 1935 the Futurists played. The following year music was provided by Mr. Boot's radiogram and there was a humorous interlude with Jim Fountain (he lived in Grange Road).

Ice creams came from Len Withey's shop in Horton View although Mrs. Withey was unable to attend in person. The day ended in traditional manner with dancing to the Ken Prewer Band in St. Hugh's Hall

Two years later and the fete occasion was made more notable by the appearance of Mrs. Gillett of Woodgreen who performed the opening ceremony. That the event took place at all was due to the willingness of the church to pay between £1 and £2 to have the grass cut at Springfields.

Fetes were usually given colour and character by the inclusion of a procession from the church hall to the hotel by Mrs Salter's band.

Fetes over the years included a baby show. In 1937 it was judged by doctors Briggs and Wharton, supported by Nurse Horton Smith who lived in Bloxham Road.

Between 1939 and 1957, priests came and departed at regular intervals. A more settled spell followed in the shape of the Rev. Goddard and Rev. Staff. It was then that there were some very notable events in the field at the rear of St. Hughs. In particular bonfire parties brought out the best in community spirit. Stan Brown would cut the grass, the cuttings from which topped up the fire. Jesse his wife and Elsie Payne made endless pickled onions for the hot dogs which were washed down with soup and coffee.

Fireworks were normally kept in a huge tub and this was fine until one year the Rev. Dennis Staff inadvertently dropped a sparkler into the mass of other fireworks. The outcome was instant and dramatic – the quickest display on record – barely time for Stan's guy to catch light.

These sorts of parties made money which was used to support Christmas events for the Sunday School

During the time that St. Hugh' had this field not all of the space was free for use. In one corner was a lawn tennis court with an associated club. It was certainly going strong in the 1940s.

St Hugh's Hall was home to many indoor and church related events. Below and on the next page are two childrens events from the early 1970s.

Auctions of jumble happened monthly on a Friday with Stan Brown as auctioneer. He stood on a chair and was confronted by bidders from right across Banbury – people who had seen the advertisement in either the Banbury Guardian or Banbury Advertiser newspapers. Only hard work secured items for this event. 'Gran' Claridge together with Elsie Payne and Jesse Brown would take a handcart round the houses of Easington. As Dennis Staff whimsically observed they were Mrs. Steptoe with her two daughters.

Saturday morning mini-markets also helped raise money. Stalls were let to anyone on the understanding that some of the takings went to the church.

Members of the Women's Fellowship were especially associated with the Michaelmas Fairs. Much jam and marmalade was made, pickled onions prepared and dolls stitched together. In fact for a while before such a fair Jesse Brown's house turned into a centre for a cottage industry in the construction of dolls from flannels.

At the fairs themselves there would be four big stalls down each side of the hall as well as a fancy dress parade.

In the fifties and sixties St. Hugh's had an active youth club. Its success owed much to a Norman Comport (he worked for Stones) and afterwards Dennis Payne

St. Hugh's Womens' Fellowship with the Rev. Robertson-Glasgow (Vicar 1947-1950). The photo also includes Mrs. Everson and her daughter Wendy, Mrs. Eeles, Mrs. Parker, Mrs. Newman, Mrs. Austin, Mrs Smith, and Mrs Brooks.

and Brian Hall. Two outstanding youth club events were a dinner and a walk. The former raised money for leukaemia and was attended by Mrs. Marten, wife of the M.P. Neil Marten. The walk was a real long distance affair – Edinburgh to Banbury. Radio Caroline covered the event which prompted Browns of Parsons street to bake Banbury Cakes for the Provost. Walkers included Brian Hall and Pete Edge.

Until at least the early 1960s St. Hugh's Hall had a very good choir. Notable members included Peter Claridge; Malcolm, Derek and Barry Heaton and Robert and Ronald Sangster.

The Rev. Goddard in particular was perceptive in the way he saw connections between different aspects of church life. For instance a Tuesday Pram Service provided valuable support for the growth of the Sunday school.

St. Hugh's Nativity Play in the early 1970s.

Life at St. Hugh's Church has been illuminated in years past by several personalities. Stan Brown has already been mentioned but there was also Albert (Bert) Wain who enjoyed a close association, especially while he was caretaker at Banbury Grammar School and then Banbury School.

The Autumn Fair owed much to Bert and he appears to have been a prime mover in the introduction of whist. A minute of 1952 called for the holding of a drive and the procuring of cards and pads.

Within the wider neighbourhood Bert and Ethel Wain were very well known and respected, so it was no surprise when they were proclaimed pearly king and queen of Springfield Avenue at the 1977 Royal Silver Jubilee celebrations.

Harriers Ground School

On July 21st 1949 Mary Cheney, who was Mayor of Banbury, officially opened Harriers Ground School on the land which was formerly Banbury Harrier's Sports Ground. Remarkably this was the first primary school to be opened locally since 1912. In the 1930s there had been some discussion about constructing an infant school in Easington Road but the land was deemed inadequate. Towards the end of that decade plans were in hand for a neighbourhood school but these were held in check when war clouds loomed. Plans were eventually prepared to open a school in the September of 1948

The opening of Harriers Ground School's swimming pool. Carol Brown is helped into the pool by Neil Marten M.P. after the opening ceremony.

The staff at Harriers Ground School about 1973. *Back row* - left to right: Anne Gascoigne, Willie Arnold, Nancy Jennings, Barry Davis, Michael Ridout, Muriel Bacon, Olive Almond. *Front row* – left to right: Jan Talbot, Gwyneth Gelling, Maggie Campbell, Jack Walpole (headteacher), Mrs. Walls, Mary Russell, Jean Westman.

For a school that had experienced so much delay in its establishment, County Circular 7101, issued to prospective parents in July 1948, must have seemed the final blow. Collisons the builders were not going to complete the building work until after the Christmas holidays.

In the meantime the embryo Harriers School occupied the ground floor of the Marlborough Road Methodist Church premises.

The Harriers School of 1949 was designed for 250 children up to the age of 11 taken from a catchment area which embraced the Easington Estate. There were six classrooms, school hall, dining hall, kitchen, cloakrooms and staff block. Later further classrooms and a swimming pool were added.

Harriers school fete, 1986.

Mrs. Campbell's Class about 1973.

Children doing art work in 1973.

Children working on word games in 1973.

Banbury School

The origins of Banbury School can be traced to Marlborough Road in 1893 but the site in the municipal buildings became inadequate for an expanding institution and a new building was developed in Ruskin Road, Easington during 1930, at a cost of £32,000.

At the time fire broke out in early February 1940, there were 351 County School pupils and 204 pupils from Fulham County School in London who were evacuated to Banbury.

Controlling the outbreak of fire was made difficult by poor water pressure. The brigade had to resort to an emergency underground tank in Springfield Avenue. Water also came from the reservoir beneath the Oxford Road water tower.

Banbury County School, now the Stanbridge Hall part of Banbury School.

The distance from the school was spanned with some hose from the Horton Hospital. Men living locally acted as volunteers in support of the brigade.

Amongst the items lost in the fire was a presentation portrait of Mr. Luscombe, the headmaster prior to Mr. Rose. Overall it took nineteen hours to control the fire.

In the aftermath of the fire St. Hugh's Hall was used by pupils of Fulham School.

The interior of the geography room.

The interior of the art room.

Easington Modern Boys School later to become the Wykham Hall part of Banbury School.

The concrete water tower that replaced the Victorian brick tower and used to supply water for the fire at Banbury School where it can be seen being demolished.

BANBURY COUNTY SCHOOL

Athletic B.C.S. Sports

SATURDAY, MAY 8th, 1937 - 2 p.m.

JUDGES—Dr. F. Davis, Messrs. G. W. White, W. H. Naylor, J. R. Railton, Misses J. M. Burwash, H. Haclin, M. Wood, H. M. Thomas

REFEREE—Mr. C. R Palmer.   STARTER—Mr. O. E. Claydon.

TIMEKEEPERS—Messrs. S. Todd and A. P. Bowran.

COMPETITORS' STEWARDS—J. H. Broome, K. Mills, B. Bliss, K. Cowley.

SPORTS COMMITTEE—Headmaster, Senior Mistress, House Masters, House Mistresses, Mr. O. E. Claydon, Miss J. M. Burwash, House Captains.

HON. SEC.—Mr. W. Mardon.

CUPS AND MEDALS FOR COMPETITION.

BOYS—Individual Championship; Runner-up; Junior Championship; Mile Challenge; Mardon (¼, ½, 1 Mile); H. H. Jones' Cup.

GIRLS—Individual Championship; Runner-up; Patterson (Junior Championship); Kate Potts (220 yds.)

OFFICERS OF HOUSES.

House	House Officers	Boy Captain	Girl Captain
Compton	Mr. W. H. Naylor Miss H. Haclin	W. Wyatt	J. Hutchinson
St. Hugh	Dr. F. Davis Miss J. M. Burwash	J. B. Johnston	D. Cotterill
Stanbridge ...	Mr. G. H. White Miss M. Wood	J. French	B. Bliss
Wykham	Mr. W. Mardon Miss H. M. Thomas	E. C. G. Jelfs	I. Lonsdale

House Officers for Compton also: Mr. A. P. Bowran; St. Hugh: Mr. J. R. Railton; Stanbridge: Mr. S. Todd; Wykham: Mr. O. E. Claydon.

SCHOOL RECORDS.
BOYS.

Event	Holder	Date	Record
100 Yds. O.	J. B. Johnston	1936	10 4/5 secs.
	C. Bailey	1928	
¼ Mile. O.	E. E. Oakes	1934	57 4/5 secs.
½ Mile. O.	S. L. Chamberlain	1934	2 m. 12 secs.
1 Mile. O.	R. Cuss	1931	5 m. 5 secs.
Hurdles. O.	L. Allen	1926	16 secs.
High Jump. O.	J. Francis	1933	5 ft.
Long Jump. O.	C. Bailey	1927	18 ft. 9½ in.
Cricket Ball. O.	W. D. Rolls	1933	86 yds.

GIRLS.

Event	Holder	Date	Record
100 Yds. O.	C. Ivens	1932	12 secs.
	J. Hutchinson	1935	
		1936	
220 Yds. O.	C. Ivens	1931	29 secs.
High Jump. O.	G. E. Marlow	1935	4 ft. 5 in.
Low Hurdles. O.	J. Hutchinson	1936	14 4/5 secs.
Cricket Ball. O.	J. Braithwaite	1934	55½ yds.

Programme—Price 3d.

The front cover of the 1937 Athletics Sports programme.

Prior to 1937, Banbury County School Sports day had been held on a Tuesday. The switch to Saturday encouraged more entries and better support. After the war there was a return to mid-week sports days.

At 2.00 p.m. over eight hundred entrants gathered in competition to assert the supremacy of their school house – Compton, St. Hughs, Stanbridge and Wykham. A fine cold May 8th was the occasion for a pupil called Johnston to create a school record for the senior quarter mile; his time of 57.2 seconds was three fifths of a second better than the previous best.

Overall fifty events were listed in the programme card priced at 3d. The final line of this was a reminder to take tea in the School Hall. There the staff, competitors, parents and friends would have watched the presentation of awards by Mrs. J. Cheney, Banbury's Mayoress.

Later that Summer, a September day was made notable by a fathers' and boys' cricket match. There were several memorable moments especially when the headmaster was bowled by his son and the mayor hit the ball so hard that he broke a stump at the other end.

The close of the Autumn Term in 1937 was characterised by special parties for junior and senior pupils. There was drama of a kind with historical and topical presentations. John Cheney the Mayor was depicted in the art of butterfly catching – he had a keen interest in the insects. A popular and very active member of staff, Mr. Mardon played the part of queen Elizabeth 1 and entered the stage on a pantomime horse.

Norman Blinkhorn presented his film of the events of the 1936 school year and Tommy Hutchings with his Futurist Band provided music for dancing.

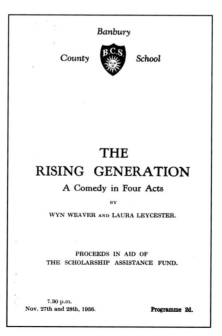

The front cover of the 1936 drama production at the County School.

Springfield House

This house stood in its own grounds in what is now Wykham Gardens. In 1920 it was the private residence of Mr. Harold Joynson but by 1931 the house is listed in Kelly's Directory as a nursing home. In 1935 it had become the property of Mr. and Mrs. S. Williams and turned into a hotel called the Springfields Hotel. It was advertised as being open to non-residents and had 4 acres of pleasure grounds with tennis, croquet and a putting green. By the end of the 1930s Mr. and Mrs. Thomas owned the hotel and during this period it became a venue for local fetes. St. Hugh's Church held their fete here on a number of occasions. Entertainment included sideshows, competitions, bowling for a pig and a children's fancy dress parade.

By the 1950s the house had become Springfields School an independent school run by Miss Mellors. In the late 1970s, early 80s the house was pulled down to build private housing.

Springfield House in the mid 1930s after becoming a hotel. Later to become a school.

SPRINGFIELDS SCHOOL

BANBURY, OXON

Boarding and Day School

Separate Kindergarten Department

Specialities — Elocution and Individual Teaching

PREPARATION FOR ALL EXAMINATIONS

Prospectus from Secretary — 'Phone Banbury 2389

Recreation and Sport

Banbury Horticultural Society

The Banbury Horticultural Society was founded in 1950 but it was not until 1984 that the Annual Open and Chrysanthemum shows were held at St. Hugh's Hall in Easington. Within two years Annual General Meetings were occupying the same venue. At the gathering of 1986 the decision was taken to encourage a wider entry to the October event by renaming it the Autumn Show. In addition to the established awards, such as the Charles Hunt Cup and the H. R. Alcock Shield, there was now scope to make a special mention of any noteworthy achievement. Bert Wain of Springfield Avenue was complimented for his arrangements of a handicraft stall – 'a good idea'.

New features were beginning to enliven the Society's events at St. Hugh's. There was the Spring Show but also a single flower competition for each meeting. Bill Larner and Bert Wain agreed to run a small raffle so as to build up a reserve of finance as a counterpoise to the Autumn Show losses.

By 1993 show costs were creating problems. The October/November show was discontinued and the September one held later in the month with an increased number of classes. Within four years there was provision for novice classes and each member was given five dwarf sunflower seeds as an encouragement to pot culture. By this time, however, the Autumn event had slipped away from Easington and moved into Marlborough Road Church Hall. Space at St. Hugh's had been limited but also a town centre location was more in the 'public eye'. In 1999 the society returned once more to St. Hugh's.

Allotments and Easington Allotment Holders Association

The cultivation of allotments has been and continues to be an important recreational activity in Easington. For a brief time just after the Second World War, there were a few plots on land adjacent to the Easington Hotel in the Bloxham Road. Lew Gray had one of these and recalls a hot summer day when the landlord of the hotel spotted him digging and emerged to offer a free pint of beer. This allotment patch eventually disappeared beneath two pairs of police houses.

The most important areas for amenity gardening have been close to Springfield Avenue and off St. Anne's Road. Originally the former was land in the ownership of the Holbech family of Farnborough House whose name was linked to the children's ward of the Horton Hospital.

Lew Grays' second home is his allotment on the Springfield Avenue site. Since 1979 this has been under the direction of the Easington Association of Allotment Holders of which he is the chairman. This association does the negotiations with Cherwell District Council and makes available seeds and fertilisers. At the outset of their existence the annual rent per plot was £5. However the financial state of the association did make it possible for allotment holders to enjoy a rent of £1 in 1986-1987.

Bert Wain admiring an exhibit at one of the Horticultural Society Shows.

Lew Gray, Chairman of the Allotment Holders Association, at work on his plot in Springfield Avenue.

A few years earlier there was much protracted discussion about the provision of a hut as well as concern regarding both poorly cultivated and vacant plots. In 1981, in the absence of a waiting list, unoccupied spaces were advertised in the Timms Road news agency.

The main attractions of allotment cultivation have been the production of fresh vegetables and the opportunity to keep physically active. During World War II some pigs were kept in sties and since then has come the occasional request to keep hens, rabbits and bees.

The Springfield Avenue site especially has survived periodic threats to the persistence of allotment culture. Between 1939 and 1945 there was an ever present danger of trespass as witness the sign discovered on the site by Arthur Coleman.

NOTICE.

DEFENCE REGULATIONS.

THIS LAND IS CULTIVATED AS ALLOTMENT GARDENS. NOTICE IS HEREBY GIVEN THAT IF ANY PERSON TRESPASSES ON THIS LAND HE SHALL UNDER REGULATION 61 (2) OF THE DEFENCE REGULATIONS, BE GUILTY OF AN OFFENCE AGAINST THIS REGULATION AND LIABLE, ON SUMMARY CONVICTION, TO A FINE NOT EXCEEDING

£50

ISSUED BY THE
NATIONAL ALLOTMENTS SOCIETY LTD
AYTON HOUSE, GORDON STREET, LONDON, W.C.1

In 1968, when Lew Gray had plot 27, there was a proposal to erect garages and these were expected to encourage houses in their wake.

Today Lew is one of sixty tenants, six of whom are ladies. Senior citizens make up a quarter of those involved. The plots are not exclusive to Easington based holders. Five come from Bloxham village, one from Grimsbury and one lives on Bretch Hill, a post war housing estate.

The other major area of plots, off St. Annes Road, is controlled directly by Cherwell District Council. Back in 1986 there was some discussion about a local association or indeed a merger of interests with the Springfield avenue group but nothing came of this.

Easington Sports

In 1997 Easington Sports Club celebrated fifty years of existence. Its formation was a post World War II move to provide for the recreational needs of the younger end of the district age range. Many potential recruits were in the process of being demobbed.

Nicknamed 'the Clan' this club adopted a multi sports approach – soccer, cricket and tennis. However football soon reigned supreme and games were against the teams of the Oxfordshire Junior League.

The season 1947-1948 was spent on some rough pasture off the Wykham Lane with a Nissan hut as changing space and water brought from a nearby brook. Matches there were all about the hustle and bustle of Section C of the Banbury Division of the Oxfordshire Junior League. Except for the company side of Switchgear, opponents were village sides like Mollington and Northend.

The Easington Sports Team of the 1953-1954 season. They were winners of the Intermediate Cup beating Quarry Nomads 2 0 in the final. They also won the Brackley Cup. *Left to right standing:* H. J. West (Trainer), F. Maycock, P. Buckle, C. Callow, M. Adkins, J. Friday. *Kneeling:* R. Vine, F. Neville, G. Anderson, (Capt.), D. Newman, B. Collett, J. Truss.

Easington Sports Team in the mid 1960s photographed before a home game. *Standing left to right:* Ike Stevens, Pete Joyner, Gerry Bayliss, Tony Tebbuts, Dickie Briggs, Frank Maycock (Secretary). *Sitting left to right:* Fred Parish, Mick Garrett, George Brain, Chick O'Leary, Georgie Moon, Mick Reynolds.

Easington Sports in the 1970s. *Standing left to right:* Mick Lancaster (Treasurer), Pete Buckle, Jimmy Thomas, Gerry Bayliss, John Gadd, Fred Parish, Frank Maycock (Secretary). *Kneeling left to right:* Barry Gill, Wilf Wilkins, Ken Richardson, George Brain, Chick O'Leary, Mick Garrett.

By the season 1954-1955 Easington Sports F.C. had acquired Oxfordshire Senior League status. Not surprisingly, at the ninth annual dinner held at the Easington Hotel in June 1955, much of the talk was about acquiring some land at Addison Road and erecting a clubhouse. Councillor Hunt, Easington F.C.s president, promised financial help. The proposed site was owned by a Wantage man called Hemmings. It had been good for barley but in the early days of soccer it gained a reputation for too much stone and not enough grass.

During the season 1959-1960 Warwickshire Combination sides like Aston Villa 'A' complained about the surface on which they were expected to play.

Ground quality was again an issue in 1970 when the Hellenic League admitted Easington F.C. One of the many outstanding achievements of that wonderful clubman Terry Horley was to use a touch of guile and a deal of fertiliser in order to achieve the greensward needed to pass inspection.

Thirty years on, programmes still welcome visitors for Hellenic League contests. The journey through the different leagues owes much to Terry but also a great deal to people like Gordon Fivash and Bob Cobill.

Gordon was the player who netted five in the 6-2 win over Northend, back in the uncertain late nineteen forties when spectators headed for Wykham Lane. This same legendary goal poacher had become honorary secretary by the time wine glasses were raised to a successful 1954-1955 season and thoughts were turning towards Addison territory.

Bob Cobill was really a rugby and hockey man but made a significant contribution to the Easington club as a grounds-man and fundraiser. His skill in marking out the pitch was a legacy of his days with the Banbury Twenty Cricket Club in the sixties.

Amongst the other club stalwarts was Tim Fountain who lived in Grange Road and was on the local V.E. day photograph. Tim was a post office engineer but was better known as an entertainer. His sketches were presented in association with Bob Arnold, Tom Forrest in the 'Archers'.

Springfield Rangers

This was a team made up of young people living in the Springfield Avenue and Easington area. Below is the team of 1952 pictured in the Easington Recreation Ground in Easington Road.

Back row left to right: Dai Williams, John Brown, Archie Buzzard, Gerry Bayliss, Mike Guy, Frank Taylor, Cyril Angell. *Front row left to right:* Bill Parish, Terry Williams, Ivan Lofthouse, Derek Anthistle, Don Hounslow.

Northern Aluminium Sports Ground

A lease of 1924 drawn up by Banbury Borough Council reveals the presence of a sports field close to Horton View.

With the coming to the town of the Northern Aluminium Company (N.A.C.) in the early 1930s this field passed into their ownership and subsequently was used for a variety of events. These included the annual athletic sports meet of N.A.C. started in 1947.

The Ladies Obstacle race in 1948

Part of the large crowd of 3,000 people enjoying the events on July 9th 1955.

Inspection team in the 1955 Tug of War against Development. *Left to right:* W. Fletcher, D. Gibbard, N. Davis, G. Joines, and the remaining people (order unknown) V. Moss, D. Haskins, S Wright, T. Coulson.

The Presentations. *Left to right are:* R. Hamer, Mrs. Whittle, Bill Whittle, J. Harrison, ?, Mrs Frazer-Bruce, Eric Ashley, Stan Fisher, Vic Harrison, Mr. Frazer-Bruce.

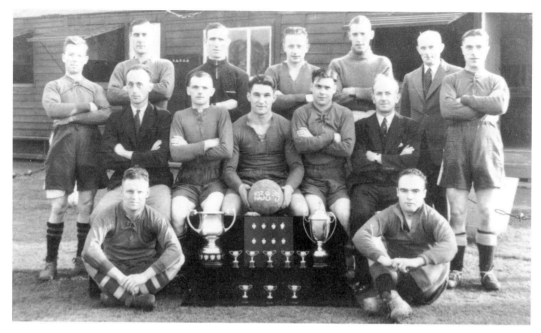

The Northern Aluminium Company's Football Team for the season 1938-1939.

Dashwood Road Primary School also used the field for its sports days and over the years the ground has been used for many different events. These include athletics, football, cricket, tennis, rugby, and bowls.

In 1936 Banbury Rugby Club showed interest in the ground at a time when they were trying to establish a permanent home. However, the ground remained with the aluminium company who in 1953 provided a new pavilion.

A game of rugby in progress, the houses of Farmfield Road are in the background.

That same year Oxfordshire Cricket Club staged its Minor Counties August fixture with Berkshire on this ground. The 27th and 28th were two remarkable days at Horton View. Overall 1,077 runs were scored. Oxfordshire achieved the highest innings total of 357 for 7 declared and yet lost by a single wicket. Berkshire were crowned champions.

Perhaps it is fortuitous that during the summer of the previous season, the company had installed the only mechanical scoreboard in the county. What is more it had been designed and fabricated in the aluminium works.

On a more frivolous note there can have been few sports grounds anywhere to have been invaded by a runaway draught horse. A Co-op milk cart was hauled at top speed around the ground by the last ever horse in their service. Clearly the horse valued its freedom as much as generations of sportsmen and women have valued the field off Horton View.

Special Occasions

Events in Easington have been special for many reasons. In 1922 there were at least two notable occasions on Harriers Field: a carnival which was part of a town shopping festival and the adoption of a new home by Banbury Harriers Football Club.

On Tuesday 30th May 1922, a Harriers based carnival was the culmination of a procession and was one of a wide range of events held in celebration of Banbury's Shopping Festival.

There was a charge of 8d (children half price) to gain access to the field but all the entertainment was free. There was Morris Dancing, music played by the combined Banbury Borough and British Legion Bands and there was a demonstration of conjuring tricks by Signor Valento. Space within the field was allowed for an old time and fancy dress cricket match involving members of the Early Closers Athletic Club.

SHOPPING CARNIVAL
ENTERTAINMENTS PROGRAMME

(Proceeds to be devoted to Charities of Town).

Thursday, May 25th, at 12 noon. Opening Ceremony by Lady Williams, accompanied by Sir Rhys Williams, M.P., and Mayor and Corporation.

7.30. Promenade Concert, Banbury Borough and British Legion Band.

Friday, May 26. Banbury Revels, 6.30 and 7.30 p.m.

Monday, May 29. Dance (arranged by Mr. W. Stroud), proceeds to be handed to Entertainment Funds.

Tuesday, May 30th. Pageant and Carnival.

Wednesday, May 31st. Banbury Revels, 6.30 and 7.30 p.m.

ıllection for Horton

On June 1st, instead of 6.30 and 7.30 p.m., Banbury Revels, there will be a Promenade Concert, at 7.30, by the Banbury Borough and British Legion Band.

Saturday 2nd, 1922 was a key date in local soccer. A footballer by the name of Russell led out the Banbury Harriers on their brand new ground off the Bloxham Road. The match was against Headington, a village suburb of Oxford, and ended 5-2 to the homesters (a reporters' buzz word in the 1920s). As the Banbury Guardian cartoonist remarked 'although Headington lost the football, the Harriers compensated them at tea'. This was laid on at the White Horse Inn in the High Street; a Smoking Concert and songs by the Bohemian Concert Party followed tea.

PLAN OF THE SHOPPING **WEEK CARNIVAL** GROUND
EASINGTON.

Apart from Jack Williamson other team members were West, Hadlington, Amis, Fosbury, Weller, Jones, Buzzard, Herbert, Wells, Hutchings, Russell, Stannard and Allen.

BANBURY HARRIERS.

(Established 1879).

President - LORD NORTH.

1923-4.

Football .. Programme

Saturday, October 6th.

HEADQUARTERS: White Horse Hotel.
GROUND: Bloxham Road.
COLOURS: Black and White Hoops.
HON. SEC.: F. Rawlings,
Vineyard Nursery,
Neithrop.
ASST. HON. SEC.: C. Shrimpton,
1, Millington Cottages,
Broughton Road.
COMMITTEE:
Messrs. E. Fosbury, E. Callow, F. Wollams, H. E. Olds, T. Barnes, T. Reedy.

OUR LITTLE CHAT—BEFORE THE MATCH.

Next week we hope to introduce a new feature in our match programme. In it you will find the fixtures of our Senior and Junior teams, results to date, and such items of interest as it is possible to give in the space at our disposal. In commencing this new feature the committee would like to take this opportunity of thanking our numerous friends for the generous support accorded to us in past seasons. Though many of last season's prominent players have left us, they have confidence that those signed on will be giving a good account of themselves shortly.

So far, our boys have not been very successful, but new men must get used to one another's play before showing their best form. On Saturday last a welcome improvement was shown and the first win was recorded. Two points from Stone's, away, was really good work and will add interest to to-day's game.

Cowley are the League champions and will be a hard nut to crack. Last season we lost the game by seven goals to one. Let us hope that a good sporting game will be seen and may the best team win. Our boys may be relied upon to put up a good show.

Next Saturday, October 13th, we entertain Abingdon Pavlova in the first round (qualifying competition) of the Amateur Cup. This will be one of the "Games of the Season"; so book the date.

SENIOR LEAGUE. TEAMS.

HARRIERS. Colours: Black and White Hoops.

R.

P. PLESTER.

L.

N. ABEL.

T. C. WOOTTON.

E. HORAN.   D. MELLIS.   R. FOUNTAIN.

W. RUSH.   H. D. WILLS.   J. W. ABEL.   P. COLLINGRIDGE   H. J. MOLD.

O

E. ALLEN.   F. J. MORRIS.   A. NASH.   P. MARTIN.   O. DRUCE.

J. E. CLARKE.   A. ALLEN.   E. GRUNDY.

A. SELWOOD.   A. R. NUTT.

L.   R. THORNTON.   R.

COWLEY. Colours: White Shirts, Blue Knickers.

KICK-OFF, 3-15 p.m.

Some People Say—

Meadow's "Rush" last Saturday reminded them of the old saying: "Where there's a Will(s) there's a way."

Ben played a cool game near the "Fountain."

Yes! we have a good goalie too.

Don't forget "Our" Dance at the Town Hall to-night.

PRICE - ONE PENNY.

Football Programme for Banbury Harriers, October 6th 1923.

HARRIERS v. MORRIS MOTORS.

Banbury Guardian, Thursday 2 April, 1921.

Cartoons by the artists F.D. Coles and F. Price were regular features throughout the seasons 1920–21 and 1921–22. Two illustrations of Harriers matches are shown.

WITH COMPLIMENTS

FROM

H. Pratt & Sons,

56, High Street, - Banbury.

Football Knickers		Football Hose
Navy or White		Any stripe tops
2/-, 2/3 and 2/6 a pair.		1/6, 2/- and 2/6 a pair.

Fanny Walden Match Ball, 20/- complete.
Tuphine Leather.
Facile Princeps, Hide Leather, **15/6** each.
Defender   ,,   ,,   **10/6** each.
Shin Guards, 1/-, 1/3 and **1/9** per pair.

SEND FOR ILLUSTRATED LIST.

Senior League Fixtures—1923-1924.

(Home team mentioned first.)

Sept. 1.—Banbury Works v. Morris Motors
          Harriers v. Chipping Norton
          Witney v Banbury G.W.R.
          Cowley v. Stones' Athletic
          Thame v. Headington
          St. Frideswide v. Bicester
Sept. 8.—Banbury G.W.R. v. Thame
          Stones' Athletic v. Headington
          Chipping Norton v. Banbury Works
          Bicester v. Banbury Harriers
          Cowley v. Morris Motors
          Oxford R.S. v. St. Frideswide

Front cover of the Oxfordshire Senior League Fixtures for 1923-1924 supplied by H. Pratt and Sons and printed by the 'Advertiser' Printing Works, Banbury.

Harriers Football Team - winners of the Banbury Charity Cup for the season 1935-1936. *Back row - left to right:* Ewert Medley (Treasurer), F. Rawlings (Secretary), T. Douglas, R. Atherton, H. Root, E. Haynes, C. Callow, R. Smith, T. Callow, W. Pennemore. *Front row - left to right:* L. Tustain, A. Knight, H. Poulton (Capt.), R. Watkinson (Vice Capt.), C. Herbert, H. Heritage.

Banbury Harriers Athletic Club about 1909.

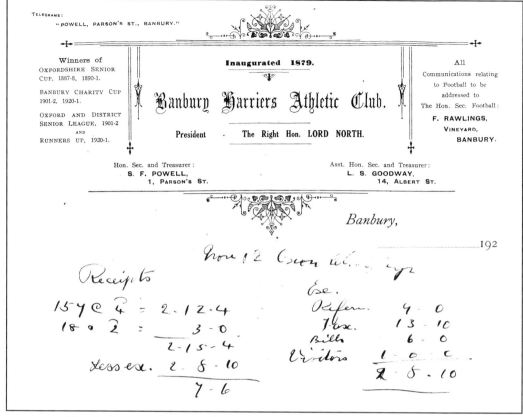

Headed notepaper for the football section of Banbury Harriers.

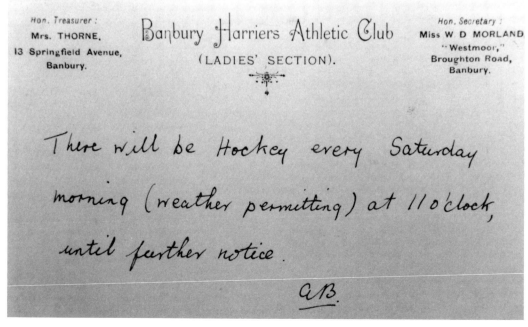

A postcard sent to the Misses Sealey in Newlands Road.

BANBURY HARRIERS' ATHLETIC CLUB

Established 1879.

President - - RIGHT HON. LORD NORTH.

FORTY-THIRD ANNUAL

Athletic Sports

(Under A.A.A., S.C.A.A.A., W.A.A.A. and N.C.U. Rules, Laws and Regulations)

Whit-Monday, June 6th, 1927

On the BANBURY HARRIERS' ATHLETIC CLUB GROUND

Judges:

W. J. BLOXHAM, Esq.	The Rev. CANON JONES.
Major S. P. YATES.	Major H. C. MAUL.
W. W. TROLLEY, Esq.	Capt. COURAGE.
C. W. FORTESCUE, Esq.	A. PARGETER, Esq.
Capt. M. W. EDMUNDS.	F. W. YOUNG, Esq., J.P.

Referee—S. J. MAWLE, Esq.

Lap Scorers—Messrs. F. RAWLINGS and G. J. STANNARD.

Timekeepers—Messrs. J. H. THOMAS and H. G. RUSSELL.

Programme Steward—Mr. H. E. OLDS.

Competitors' Stewards—Messrs. W. PARKER, C. SHRIMPTON and C. CASTLE.

Committee Tent Steward—Mr. G. TALBOT.

Ground Steward—Mr. E. HOBBS.

Starter—Mr. J. E. ATHERSUCH.

Committee—

Mrs. Bird, Mrs. Stannard, Mrs. Eyre, Mrs. S. Lester, Mrs. Busby, Mrs. Betts, Miss Morland, Miss Bonham, Messrs. A. Parker, T. Reedy, G. Taplin, J. H. Thomas, B. R. Morland, H. E. Olds, F. Rawlings, H. Lay, C. Viggers, T. Langley, G. Talbot, J. Keen, H. Harris.

Treasurer—Mr. H. EYRE.

Hon. Secretary—Mr. W. G. MASCORD.

Assistant Secretary—Mr. S. F. POWELL.

The PRIZES will be distributed immediately after the Sports by Mrs. J. A. Gillett, Mayor of Banbury.

Programme—THREEPENCE.

"Advertiser" Press, Banbury.

In 1925, the Banbury Harriers Athletic Club regarded their ground as offering 'a splendid view over the surrounding country'.

Harriers ground witnessed many exciting events. Not the least of these was the Athletic Sports Club's meeting of the midsummer of 1925. Quite apart from the usual races that were watched by a huge crowd, there was the special attraction of a performer on a trapeze who used the professional names Fitzroy and Katz. He fluctuated between imitating Tarzans flying ape and filling the role of Felix on the flying rings.

The Oxfordshire Agricultural Show in the early part of the 20th century.

An annual event held in fields bordering Wykham Lane was the Oxfordshire Agricultural Show. In the May of 1937 Easington was the scene of great activity with a show ground near the county school. Banbury was thought to be a good location as the town was accessible from Northampton and Warwick.

Early stages of preparation had been handicapped by water logging but, despite this, 1937 saw a record entry of cattle and goats, the latter having appeared for the first time in 1933. Over one hundred implements and trade exhibitions were included in the biggest display of its kind since 1925.

Banbury Amateur Operatic Society

A significant venue for special events in the district has been Banbury School's Wykham Hall, formerly known as Easington Modern Boys School. Apart from 1964, all the productions of the Banbury Amateur Operatic Society (B.O.A.S.) have been held there.

The origins of B.O.A.S. can be traced back to the 1961 presentation of the Pirates of Penzance. This was the outcome of collaboration between the Banbury Cross players and Easington Boys School located at the end of Ruskin Road.

Two leading parts, the Pirate King and Mabel were played by Stanley and Gladys Blackler. These enthusiasts of song and dance routines had brought their keenness and determination from earlier experiences in the North of England.

By the Autumn of 1966 when the production was The Gondoliers the society had become well established and certain key faces had been imprinted on the Banbury operatic scene. Dickie Briggs was a good example of someone who had already made his mark as a member of the Old Banburians Dramatic Society and the Banbury Cross players.

A scene from the first production of the Pirates of Penzance in 1961.

Like Dickie, Gareth Jeremy was a founder member of the B.O.A.S as was Jennifer Powell (Tustain) who had been Gianetta in the Gondoliers. Thomas Pratt took the part of Guiseppe Palmieri in the same show. Like Jeremy, he has gone on to give much pleasure to audiences for many years.

In marked contrast to 'The Pirates', Wykham stage 2000 was occupied by 'Annie Get Your Gun'. Dickie and Gareth are still there but they have been joined by Sarah Thorp (Annie Oakley) eager for singin', dancin', and shootin' and Paul Clark (Frank Butler) who is Annie's man in the end but not before a whole lot of shootin'! Worthy support for these on stage came from the orchestra under its conductor David Ball. This is another tradition dating back from 1961.

The society reaches the 40th milestone in 2001 and looks set to hold many more events of its own very special brand of entertainment which will draw the people of Banbury to Easington. Stan and Gladys Blackler would have been thrilled at the prospect.

A scene from the year 2000 production of 'Annie Get Your Gun'.

The Duke of Plaza-Toro
(Cedric Senior)

The Duchess of Plaza-Toro
(Gladys Blackler)

Don Alhambra Del Bolero
(Gareth Jeremy)

Casilda
(Sonia Blinkhorn)

Marco Palmieri
(Dicky Briggs)

Gianetta
(Jennifer Powell)

Guiseppe Palmieri
(Thomas Pratt)

Tessa
(Sally Warwick)

Luiz
(Jeremy Hardwick)

Leading members of the cast for the 'Gondoliers' in 1966.

The Easington Coronation Band

The Easington Coronation Band was also known as the Easington Poorah, Kazoo or Jazz band. It was formed in 1935 for the celebrations for the Silver Jubilee of George V and was aimed at providing some form of interest or entertainment for the children of Easington. The band continued after these celebrations and took its name, the Easington Coronation band, from the Coronation celebrations for George VI.

The band increased in size and became involved in fund raising for the Horton Hospital. In 1938 in the week leading up to the Hospital Fete it toured the town advertising the fete and collecting money. It collected £20 during that week. Subsequently it won its group class in the Fete procession of that year.

The band lined up advertising the Hospital Fete.

The Easington Coronation Band marching in Springfield Avenue for the Coronation of George VI.

On November 5th 1938 the band headed a torchlight procession and collected £10 towards the Horton Hospital Building Fund. The paper reported that Guy Fawkes Night was enlivened by a torchlight procession accompanying the Easington Jazz band directed by Mrs. G. Salter which paraded the town collecting for the Horton Hospital appeal. The band returned to Easington and formed a ring round a huge bonfire on the recreation ground, which was set alight by the torchbearers at a given signal. Fully 1,000 people were present at the bonfire. In 1939 it decided to increase its size to 40 members and engagements were booked at village fetes and in the town.

In order to finance new instruments and the handmade costumes, a plea for donations was made on behalf of the committee by the secretary Mrs. Edith Salter of 40 Springfield Avenue. The committee consisted of Mrs. Blincowe President, Mrs. J. Cheney Vice-President, Mr. H. Coleman Treasurer and Mrs. Salter. Money was donated by many local residents as well as notable people of the area. For example Mary Cheney gave £1-1-0, Baron Perfumo of Avon Carrow at Avon Dassett £2-2-0. The money raised was then spent at Bernard Smith's the draper to buy material etc. The uniform was a scarlet tunic with white trousers and blue hat.

Wartime
Like all other parts of the town, Easington also did its bit during World War II. The ARP post was in the building which now houses the Post Office in Horton View. The warden in charge was C. J. Walters who lived in Horton View.

Various parts of Easington were involved in the war effort and the certificates below shows an acknowledgement for the Salute the Soldier National Savings Campaign of 1944. These were presented to part of Springfield Avenue which was divided up into sections for fund raising.

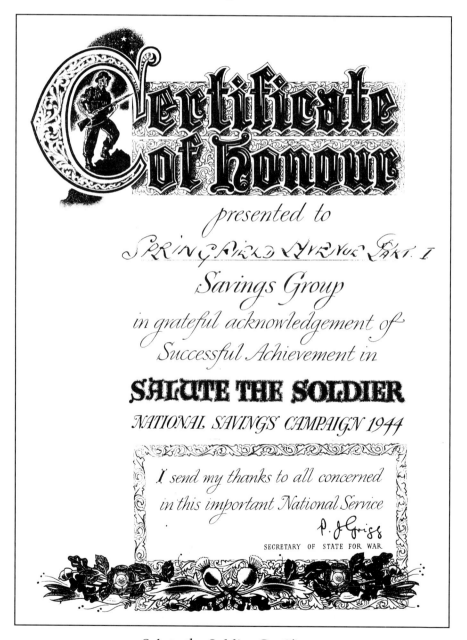

Salute the Soldier Certificate.

This photo shows some of the Easington's Civil Defence volunteers. Back centre is Mrs. Salter one of the ARP wardens for Easington.

Ambulance Volunteers c1941-1942 taken at the site of the old Ewins Garage that was off Marlborough Place next to Dashwood Road School. The ambulance volunteers are left to right: *Back row:* Joe Bliss, George Hudson, Fritz Langston *Front row:* Frank Jebbitt, Sam Brown, Alf Truss and Mark Buzzard. Mark Buzzard ran the shop at 38 Springfield Avenue and Sam Brown lived at 42 Springfield Avenue.

Members of St. Hugh's church celebrating Victory in Europe at the end of the war. Many of the children are in fancy dress.

Banbury Home Guard parading on the playing field of Banbury Grammar School now part of Banbury School.

Royal Occasions

Coronation year 1937 produced its own special events when the arrival of a new monarch was celebrated in Easington. Saturday May 15th was Children's Day. One highlight was a big fancy dress procession around the estate followed by children's sports in the recreation ground.

Tea and entertainment for 450 children took place in the Drill Hall. Events for adults were held a week later and were focussed entirely on the hall. There was a tea followed by a social and dance. Streets and buildings of this part of Banbury had attractive displays. There was a special lighting effect at the Easington Hotel. Residential properties as well as the County School in Ruskin Road were bedecked in flags and bunting.

There was entertainment, parades and parties held in the Avenue as well as Farmfield and Grange Road.

Children lined up in fancy dress in Springfield Avenue for 1937 Coronation.

Fancy dress parade in Wykham Place 1937.

Part of Springfield Avenue towards the Bloxham Road with its bunting for the 1937 Coronation.

Mr. Barnard (centre) Mrs. Salter (right) and Ken Woodward (left) entertaining at the junction of Grange Road and Springfield Avenue as part of the 1937 Coronation celebrations.

Children parading from Wykham place into Ruskin Road.

The Brown's house decked out for 1977 in Springfield Avenue.

In 1977 the area celebrated again, this time it was the Silver Jubilee of Queen Elizabeth II. In Springfield Avenue the street was decorated with bunting and became a tourist attraction with cars from other parts of the town driving up and down to see the display.

A committee was put together, permission to shut the road was granted and each household was asked to help towards the food. On the day a street parade was held and sports took place on the fields of Banbury School, but as the afternoon progressed it began to rain and the tea party had to be held in the Wykham Hall part of Banbury School.

Postscript

In common with most other parts of Banbury, the pace of recent change within the Easington district has quickened perceptibly. Banbury Rugby Club has retreated to the vast expanses of Bodicote Park. White clad figures no longer flicker to and fro at Grange Road. The Cricket Club is now also at Bodicote, leaving memories of sticky wickets to be represented by a name plaque on a property within the 'Pavilions' development of homes.

Large buses and coaches serve the needs of a greater secondary school population, but the Stagecoach successor to the Midland Red meets its public transport commitments by using a system of minibuses, whose circular route includes Bodicote Chase and Cherwell Heights as well as Easington. Long gone are the large red double decker buses that once served the area.

Small shops have persisted but have had to adapt to an age of superstore competition. John Stokes (fruit and vegetables) has just called it a day in Horton View but Michael Louch continues to find a niche for a family butcher. Meanwhile at Timms Road, Paul Taylor combines an interest in meat with a willingness to compensate for the loss of traditional bread making in Banbury and Grimsbury.

Local and corner shop news agencies continue to attract much custom through convenience and personal service. The elderly of Easington can draw pensions at a sub Post Office and the ladies of the area look to 'Elegance' for attention and hair styling. Home deliveries, apart from newspapers, are virtually confined to franchise milk arrangements in consultation with Central Midland Co-op.

Land at Bloxham Road is viewed by at least one house developer, Beazer Homes, as strategic land. This company seeks to offer a 'sustainable solution' to Banbury's town expansion needs by proposing the creation of a mixed use scheme with provision for 1250 houses.

As much as anything the story of Easington has been a tale of advancing frontiers. Successively the Oxford Road, Springfield Avenue and Sycamore Drive have provided active margins.

Will Wykham Lane become a new boundary for the early 21st Century? If this proves to be the case, Easington will have come a long way since the Bishop of Lincoln established his home farm.